The Ultimate Book of Unusual Insights

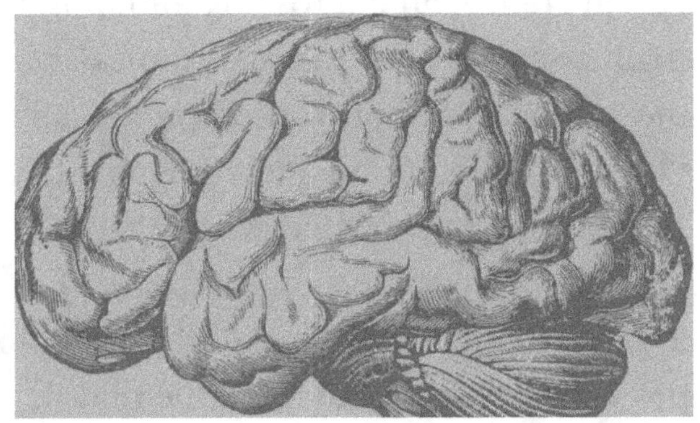

Fascinating Lesser-Known Facts and new discoveries Across Nature, Science, and Human Experience

SCOTT

KELLER

1

ABOUT THE BOOK

Dive deeply into the hidden beauties of our world with **The Ultimate Book of Unusual Insights: Fascinating Lesser-Known Facts Across Nature, Science, and Human Experience**, an engrossing anthology. This book, which covers a wide range of topics and is curated by the knowledgeable Scott Keller, provides readers a treasure trove of unexpected and enjoyable trivia.

Discover the unexpected with this book. As it covers everything from the subtle aspects of human behavior to the hidden mysteries of the animal kingdom. The stapes bone, which is found in the middle ear, is the smallest bone in the human body. Or that the Neanderthal flute, which is thought to be about 40,000 years old and fashioned from a bird's bone, is the oldest musical instrument ever discovered?

These are but a few of the amazing facts that are in store for you. Set Out on an Exploration of Knowledge Based on Science, Nature, and Human Experience

It is ideal for anyone who enjoys sharing fascinating anecdotes, is a trivia enthusiast, or is just naturally interested. It is intended to offer brief, easily assimilated information that is ideal for igniting discussions and expanding your understanding.
Take in a world of surprising discoveries and establish yourself as the authority on fascinating trivia.

Author's Notes

Dear Reader,

Greetings and welcome to **The Ultimate Book of Unusual Insights: Fascinating Lesser-Known Facts Across Nature, Science, and Human Experience**. I'm excited to share this compilation with you as a lifelong lover of the odd and the weird as well as an obsessive collector of trivia.

My love for unearthing the obscure facts that contribute to our world's amazing complexity and never-ending fascination gave rise to this book. The little things that frequently go overlooked, the revelations that give our daily lives a magical touch, and the facts that cause one to pause and reflect have always piqued my curiosity.

Every pages aims to pique your interest and deepen your comprehension, covering everything from the wonders of scientific discovery to the enigmas surrounding human behavior and the natural world. Not only did I want to educate, but I also wanted to arouse amazement and serve as a constant reminder of what an amazing world we live in.

I hope you find this book to be enjoyable and enlightening. I think you will find something here to connect with you, regardless of whether you are an experienced trivia fan, an inquisitive learner, or someone who enjoys sharing fascinating anecdotes with friends and family. Every fact provides a look into the complex and frequently unexpected nature of existence; it is a small component of a bigger picture.

May your journey through these pages bring you delight in the small things, happiness in the unexpected, and a fresh perspective on the world around you. I appreciate you coming along on this exploration journey with me. I'm thrilled to honor the wonderful web of knowledge that unites us all and to share these uncommon insights with you.

Enjoy your reading!
Sincerely,
Scott Keller

INTRODUCTION

Have you ever been fascinated by the mysteries of scientific discovery, the quirks of the natural world, or the complexities of human behavior???

You'll find solutions to queries you never even knew you had in these pages. Every fact opens a new perspective on the world around us, revealing everything from the amazing ways that plants and animals have adapted to the mysterious workings of the human body and mind.

This collection aims to revive the excitement of curiosity rather than merely impart knowledge. Every fact has been selected with care to offer a balance between the amusing and the instructive, so there is something for everyone.

Did you know that the femur is the longest bone in the human body??? And that the human brain can interpret images in as little as 13 milliseconds???

Join us on a tour through the lesser-known, where you will discover these truths and many more similar ones.

Prepare to explore, be astounded, and share these fascinating discoveries with loved ones.

Flip the page, and let the journey commence!

Facts to Know Before Engaging in This Book

Here are some tips to improve your reading experience before you start learning!!

- Welcome Your Inquisitiveness: This book is meant for the inquisitive reader. Get ready to investigate a variety of subjects, each providing a distinct window into the intriguing facets of our reality.

- Be Prepared for the Unknown: This book contains information on a wide range of topics, including human behavior, anatomy, and scientific phenomena as well as the natural environment. Every page contains a surprise for you.

- Savor Bite-Sized Education: Every fact is provided in a clear, simple-to-understand manner. Because of this, it's ideal for short reading sessions, giving you the chance to learn something new in a short amount of time.

- Discuss Your Findings:Learning these facts is enjoyable, and they also make excellent conversation starters. Please don't hesitate to impart your acquired wisdom to loved ones, coworkers, and friends.

- Broaden Your Perspective: The information provided is intended to increase your awareness of and appreciation for the world. Be open-minded and filled with amazement as you approach each one.

- Enter and Exit: It is not necessary to read this book sequentially. You are welcome to skip to any part that piques your interest. Because each fact stands alone, it's simple to investigate at your own leisure.

- Aesthetic Joy: To make the material more relatable, some facts are supplemented by pictures. Savor the visual components that go well with the words.

- Eternal Education: Think of this book as a first step in a lifetime of study. Allow it to motivate you to learn more about subjects that catch your attention.

- Remain Inquiring: Keep in mind that there are many wonders in the world just waiting to be found. Allow this book to pique your interest and motivate you to never stop posing queries and looking for solutions.

- Have Fun: Above all, make sure you enjoy yourself. Acquiring novel and peculiar knowledge ought to be an enjoyable and captivating endeavor that evokes delight and enthusiasm.

With these points at your disposal, you're prepared to go out on an adventure into the strange and unknown. I hope you have fun reading and that you come upon lots of wonderful surprises!

Table of Contents

ABOUT THE BOOK 2

Author's Notes.. 3

INTRODUCTION 5

Facts to Know Before Engaging in This Book 6

RANDOM THINGS 10

LESSER KNOWN FACTS ABOUT ANIMAL 14

LESSER KNOWN FACTS ABOUT PLANTS 24

LESSER KNOWN FACTS ABOUT HUMAN BEHAVIOUR... 34

LESSER KNOWN FACTS ABOUT PART OF THE BODY
HUMAN 44

LESSER KNOWN FACTS ABOUT SPORT 52

LESSER KNOWN FACTS ABOUT LIFE 62

LESSER KNOWN FACTS ABOUT NEW BORN BABBIES ... 72

LESSER KNOWN FACTS ABOUT CLOTHING AND SHOES 82

LESSER KNOWN FACTS ABOUT FOOD AND DRINKS 88

LESSER KNOWN FACTS ABOUT MEDICAL 92

LESSER KNOWN FACTS ABOUT MUSIC........................... 96

LESSER KNOWN FACTS ABOUT HUMAN BRAINS 100

LESSER KNOWN FACTS ABOU HUMAN REACTION 104

CONCLUSION.. 108

GLOSSARY 109

APPENDIX... 111

RANDOM THINGS

Here are a few interesting and lesser-known things:

* **Tardigrades** Also referred to as water bears, these minuscule organisms are able to endure harsh environments, such as the vacuum of space.

* When one sense is simultaneously seen as if by one or more additional senses, as in the case of hearing sounds as colors, this condition is known as **synesthesia**.

* **The Fermi Paradox** is the seeming inconsistency between the likelihood of extraterrestrial civilizations existing and the paucity of evidence supporting them.

* **The Voynich Manuscript** : A bizarre, untranslated text from the fifteenth century that features unusual diagrams, unidentified vegetation, and an untranslated language.

* **The Baader-Meinhof Phenomenon**: Also called frequency illusion, it is the appearance of what you recently learnt everywhere all of a sudden.

❖ **Cicada 3301** an online collection of challenging riddles and virtual reality games that first appeared in 2012; they are thought to have been created as a recruiting tool for those interested in cryptography.

❖ **Dyatlov Pass Incident** is The mystery that occurred in 1959 in the Ural Mountains, leaving nine Russian hikers dead for unknown reasons.

❖ **Bioluminescent Bay** Found in regions like Puerto Rico, these bays are distinguished by their large quantities of bioluminescent plankton, which causes the water to glow when disturbed.

DID YOU KNOW??

❖ The spac between your eyebrows is called glabella

❖ The way it smells after rain is called petrichor

❖ The plastic metallic quoting at the end of your shoelace is called aglet

❖ When your stomach rumbles it's called wambles

❖ The cry of a new born baby is called vagitus

- ❖ The prongs of a fork is called tines

- ❖ The sheen of light that you see when you close your eye and press your hand on them is called phosphenes

- ❖ The tiny plastic thing placed in the middle of a pizza box is called box tent

- ❖ The day over tomorrow is called overmorrow

- ❖ Your little toe or finger is called minimus

- ❖ The wired cage that holds the cork of a bottle of champagne is called a agraffe

- ❖ The 'na na na' and 'la la la' which don't really have any meaning in the lyrics of any song are called vocables

- ❖ When you combine a question mark with an exclamation mark (?!) it is referred to as an interrobang

- ❖ The space between your nostrils is called columella nasi

❖ The armhole in clothes where the sleeves are sewn is called armscye

❖ Finding it difficult to get out of bed in the morning is called dysania

❖ Illegible handwriting is called griffonage

❖ The dot over an 'i' and 'j' is called tittle

❖ That sick feeling you get after eating or drinking too much is called crapulence

❖ The metal thing used to measure your feet at the shoe store is called Bannock device

LESSER KNOWN FACTS ABOUT ANIMAL

Here are interesting and lesser-known animal phenomena and facts:

➤ The salamander species known as an **axelotl** is capable of regenerating its heart, spinal cord, limbs, and other organs.

➤ The **Turritopsis dohrnii, or "immortal jellyfish,"** is well-known for its capacity to transform back into a juvenile after reaching adulthood, thereby evading extinction.

➤ **Mimic Octopus**: Capable of mimicking the appearance and motions of over fifteen distinct marine animals, such as sea snakes, flatfish, and lionfish.

➤ **Pistol Shrimp**: Stuns or kills victims by using its claw to generate a cavitation bubble that bursts with a loud snap.

- ➢ **The Bombardier Beetle** uses its abdomen to shoot a hot chemical spray in self-defense.

- ➢ **Narwhal**: This whale, sometimes referred to as the "unicorn of the sea," has a long, spiral tusk that protrudes from its head.

- ➢ The **honey badger** is well-known for its bravery and resistance to porcupine quills, snake bites, and bee stings.

- ➢ **Platypus**: Males possess a painful spur on their rear limbs, making them one of the few venomous animals.

- ➢ **Glass Frog**: Its transparent skin makes its interior organs visible.

- ➢ **Leafcutter Ants**: These ants use leaves as a substrate to cultivate fungal gardens and demonstrate sophisticated agricultural techniques.

- ➢ The **Mantis Shrimp** is an animal with the most sophisticated vision in the animal kingdom. It can identify cancer cells and perceive polarized light.

- **Electric Eel**: Capable of producing 600 volt electric shocks to defend itself or stun prey.

- **Tardigrades** are microscopic organisms that can withstand harsh environments like radiation, starvation, and space vacuum.

- **Bowerbird**: To entice mates, male bowerbirds construct intricate buildings and embellish them with vibrant items.

- **Lungfish**: By burying itself in muck and breathing air, lungfish may live for years without water.

- **Naked Mole-Rat**: With a single breeding queen, this unique social structure is akin to that of ants and bees.

- The **pangolin** is the only mammal with keratin scale armor covering its body.

- **Archerfish**: Capable of launching water jets into the water to chase insects off branches so they can be eaten.

- **Sea cucumbers**: They have the ability to restore their internal organs after eject them as a defensive strategy.

- A fish known as a **mudskipper** is able to breathe through its skin and use its pectoral fins to walk on land.

- **Mimic Poison Dart Frog:** Though not poisonous in and of itself, it resembles the extremely dangerous poison dart frogs.

- The **Saiga Antelope** is distinguished by its large, bulbous snout, which aids in controlling body temperature and dust intake.

- One of the most ferocious birds, the **cassowary** is distinguished by its strong legs and keen claws.

- **Okapi**: This elusive mammal, also called a "forest giraffe," has stripes like zebras and a long neck.

- The **star-nosed mole** has 22 fleshy appendages that are incredibly sensitive to touch, forming a distinctive nose shaped like a star.

- **Aye-Aye**: A particular species of lemur that uses its long, slender middle finger to scrape insects from the bark of trees.

> **Velvet Worm**: Uses a sticky slime spray to entice prey, which it subsequently devours.

> Lizard known as the **"Jesus Christ Lizard"** because it can sprint on the water's surface is the basilisk.

> **Butterfly mimicry:** To elude predators, certain butterflies, such as the Viceroy, imitate the colors of poisonous species, such as the monarch.

DID YOU KNOW???

- ➢ A blue whale's tongue has the same weight as an elephant's.

- ➢ Octopuses are blue-blooded and have three hearts. An arrangement of flamingos is referred to as "flamboyance."

- ➢ Kangaroos are unable to turn around.

- ➢ Honeybees are able to identify faces.

- ➢ The tongue of a chameleon can reach a length of twice its body length.

- ➢ A shrimp's heart is found in its head. Only elephants are incapable of jumping.

- ➢ When they sleep, sea otters hold hands so they don't drift apart.

- ➢ Seven vertebrae make up a giraffe's neck, the same amount as a human's.

➤ Penguins use pebbles to ask their partners to marry them.

➤ Despite lacking brains, starfish are able to regrow missing limbs.

➤ Cows might get anxious when they are separated from their dearest companions.

➤ The British Empire and the Zanzibar Sultanate fought the shortest war in history, lasting just 38 minutes.

➤ We refer to a cluster of jellyfish as a "smack."
The fingerprints left by koalas and humans are nearly identical.

➤ A sixth "finger" that pandas have helps them grip bamboo.

➤ The largest land mammal in the world, the African elephant can weigh up to 12,000 pounds.

➤ Certain frog species have the ability to freeze during the winter and thaw out in the spring.

- Sloths climb down from trees once a week to relieve themselves.

- A camel's eyes are designed to block out sand and are capable of closing entirely.

- Water bears, or tardigrades, are able to endure in harsh conditions, such as space.

- The long, spiral tusks of narwhals are actually teeth.

- The size of a lima bean is that of a newborn kangaroo.

- Elephants use low-frequency noises to communicate over great distances.

- A salamander species that can regenerate complete limbs and even portions of the brain is the axolotl.

- Certain octopus species have the ability to alter their skin's color and texture in order to blend in with their environment.

- The fastest bird in the world is the peregrine falcon, which can dive to nearly 240 mph.

➢ Wombats mark their area and keep themselves from rolling away by forming their excrement into cubes.

➢ The only species in which the male becomes pregnant and gives birth are seahorses.

LESSER KNOWN FACTS ABOUT PLANTS

Here are interesting and lesser-known phenomena and facts about plants:

- ❖ **Rafflesia arnoldii**: Attracts pollinators with the scent of rotting flesh, producing the largest flower in the world.

- ❖ The **corpse flower**, or **Amorphophallus titanum**, may reach a height of ten feet and releases an unpleasant stench to draw pollinating insects.

- ❖ **Venus Flytrap**: A herbivorous plant that closes when prey triggers its sensitive hairs.

- ❖ **Pitcher Plant**: An additional carnivorous plant that holds insects in its digestive fluid-filled pitcher-shaped leaves.

- ❖ **Baobab Tree**: Distinguished by its enormous trunk, which has the capacity to retain millions of liters of water during dry spells.

- ❖ **Welwitschia mirabilis**: A desert plant that may survive for more than a millennium with just two leaves.

- ❖ **Massive Sequoia**: With heights of more than 300 feet, these trees are among the biggest in the world.

- ❖ **Mimosa pudica**, the sensitive plant, defends itself from herbivores by folding its leaves when they come into contact with them.

- ❖ The **Dragon's Blood Tree** (Dracaena cinnabari) yields a red sap that is used to make colors and medications.

- ❖ **Wolffia globosa**, sometimes referred to as **watermeal**, is the tiniest blooming plant on Earth.

- ❖ **Cycads** are ancient plants that have been around since the dinosaur era.

- ❖ **Titan Arum**: Like corpse flowers, it has a massive inflorescence that emits an unpleasant stench to draw pollinators.

- ❖ Some of the oldest living trees are **bristlecone pines**; some of them are over 5,000 years old.

- ❖ The feces-emitting bloom of **Hydnora africana,** a parasitic plant, attracts pollinators.

- ❖ The uncommon and endangered **Dendrophylax lindenii**, or **ghost orchid,** is an orchid with no leaves that depends on fungi for symbiosis.

- ❖ **Sosola**, or **tumbleweed**, splits off from its root and rolls in the wind to scatter its seeds.

- ❖ **Kudzu**: Also referred to as "the vine that ate the South," this plant spreads quickly and can completely cover an area.

- ❖ **Sundew (Drosera):** Carnivorous plants that catch and eat insects thanks to their sticky, glandular hairs.

- ❖ **Bamboo**: The world's fastest-growing plant, certain species can reach a height of 35 inches in a single day.

- ❖ **The corpse lily (Bulbophyllum phalaenopsis)** is another plant that attracts pollinators by giving off a potent smell of decomposition.

- ❖ **Ginkgo biloba**: Known as a **"living fossil,"** this plant hasn't changed in over 200 million years.

- ❖ The non-photosynthetic Ghost Plant (**Monotropa uniflora**) gets its nourishment from mycorrhizal fungus.

- ❖ The **saguaro cactus** is well-known for both its distinctive form and its capacity to hold a lot of water in its tissues.

- ❖ **Selaginella lepidophylla**, also known as the resurrection plant, is capable of withstanding severe dryness and reviving when water is added.

- ❖ **Strangler Fig**: Expands all around a host tree until it eventually engulfs and consumes it.

- ❖ **Lithops**: Often referred to as "living stones," these succulents eschew herbivory by becoming the shape of stones.

- ❖ With a diameter of up to three feet, the corpse plant (**Rafflesia arnoldii**) produces the largest single blossom.

* ❖ Certain **eucalyptus** species yield volatile oils that have the ability to catch fire and spread wildfires.

* ❖ **Spanish moss**, or **Tillandsia usneoides**, is an epiphyte that clings to trees and takes in moisture and nutrients from the atmosphere.

* ❖ **Theobroma cacao**, the cacao tree, yields the beans used to produce chocolate and is pollinated by tiny midges.

DID YOU KNOW???

- In a single day, bamboo can grow up to 35 inches.

- *Rafflesia arnoldii*, the largest flower in the world, has a pungent smell of rotting flesh and can reach a diameter of more than three feet.

- Strawberries are not berries; bananas are.

- *Mycorrhizal* networks, which are underground networks of fungi, allow plants to connect with one another.

- The *Venus flytrap* uses the insects it captures to break down and extract nutrition.

- The fluffy, white leaves of panda plants (Kalanchoe tomentosa) bear a resemblance to the fur of pandas.

- The trunk of a baobab tree has the capacity to hold up to 32,000 gallons of water.

- Certain plants can close their leaves in response to contact, such as the mimosa pudica.

❖ With a height of more than 379 feet, the coast redwood known as Hyperion is the tallest tree in the world.

❖ Sunflowers have flowers that turn to follow the sun, and they can reach heights of up to 12 feet.

❖ It can take a Saguaro cactus up to 200 years to produce its first limb.

❖ Not all succulents are cacti, yet cacti are nonetheless succulents.

❖ Over the course of its life, an oak tree can yield up to 10 million acorns.

❖ When the corpse flower (Amorphophallus titanum) blooms, it can take up to ten years and smells like decaying flesh.

❖ Certain plants, such as the African violet, can survive in low light.

❖ The plant aloe vera is well-known for its calming gel, which helps soothe burns and other skin irritations.

- ❖ Additionally, plants can ward off herbivores or draw in pollinators with chemical signals.

- ❖ Natural rubber is made from latex, which is produced by the rubber tree (Hevea brasiliensis).

- ❖ The jade plant (Crassula ovata) is frequently regarded as a lucky charm due to its longevity.

- ❖ Desmodium gyrans, also known as the "dancing plant," has leaves that move quickly in reaction to light and other stimuli.

- ❖ For ages, indigenous ceremonies and healing techniques have made use of psychoactive plants such as ayahuasca and peyote.

- ❖ Nepenthes, the plant that makes pitchers, has evolved to use its pitcher-shaped leaves to catch and digest insects.

- ❖ Cannabis and hemp are two separate species, however while they are related, hemp has less THC than cannabis.

- ❖ Because of its reputation for improving air quality, the bamboo palm is frequently utilized indoors.

- ❖ Compounds in aloe vera gel have been demonstrated to have antibacterial and anti-inflammatory effects.

- ❖ One of the oldest tree species, ginkgo biloba has not evolved much over the course of 200 million years.

- ❖ A red resin that is used as a dye and in traditional medicine is produced by the dragon's blood tree (Dracaena cinnabari).

- ❖ Certain plants, such as calendula, have long been utilized for their therapeutic benefits in the treatment of wounds.

- ❖ The kudzu plant is well-known for its capacity to suffocate and cover other plants. It grows incredibly quickly.

- ❖ Some plants, like nasturtium, have edible leaves and blossoms that taste like pepper that are used in salads.

LESSER KNOWN FACTS ABOUT HUMAN BEHAVIOUR

Here are interesting and lesser-known phenomena and facts about human behavior:

➢ The propensity to notice something more frequently after first learning about it is known as the **Baader-Meinhof Phenomenon.**

➢ People who are not very good at a task tend to overestimate their abilities, a cognitive bias known as the **Dunning-Kruger Effect**.

➢ **Placebo Effect**: A phenomena in which patients who get a treatment that has no therapeutic benefit but actually improves their condition.

➢ **Barnum Effect**: The propensity for people to interpret general or ambiguous words as having personal significance.

➢ **Confirmation bias** is the propensity to look for, analyze, and retain data that supports one's preconceived notions.

➢ The discomfort that arises in the mind when one or more values or beliefs are in conflict with one another is known as **cognitive dissonance**.

➢ The propensity to allow one favorable attribute to sway one's opinion of a person or something overall is known as the "**halo effect**."

➢ The **Hawthorne Effect** is when people change how they behave when they realize they are being watched.

➢ When one is concentrating on another task and fails to notice an unexpected stimulus that is right in front of them, it is known as **inattentional blindness**.

➢ The inclination to recognize recognizable patterns in random stimuli, like faces, is known as **pareidolia**.

➢ The **Pygmalion Effect** is the idea that performance rises when expectations are raised.

➢ The propensity for people to be less inclined to assist a victim in the presence of other people is known as the "**bystander effect**."

- The propensity to recall incomplete tasks more vividly than finished ones is known as the **Zeigarnik Effect**.

- Delaying or postponing work is known as **procrastination**, and it's frequently caused by a lack of drive or a fear of failing.

- **Groupthink** is the propensity for a group's decisions to be dysfunctional or unreasonable as a result of harmony and conformity demands.

- The phenomenon known as the "**mere exposure effect**," in which people form preferences for something just because they are accustomed to them.

- **Anchoring Bias**: The propensity to base judgments unduly on the first piece of information one comes across.

- **Self-serving** bias is the propensity to place the blame for unfavorable results on outside forces and to ascribe positive outcomes to oneself.

- **Fundamental Attribution Error**: The propensity to overemphasize personal traits and disregard contextual cues when assessing the actions of others.

- ➢ **Social Loafing**: The propensity for people to work less hard in a group setting than they would alone.

- ➢ **False Consensus Effect**: The propensity to exaggerate the degree to which one's own views, attitudes, and actions are shared by others.

- ➢ **Erroneous Arousal Attribution**: When individuals incorrectly assign their innate arousal to an incorrect origin.

- ➢ The propensity to exaggerate how much other people observe and assess our conduct and appearance is known as the **"spotlight effect."**

- ➢ The inclination to stick with a project because of the total amount invested in the past, even when fresh information indicates that doing so will cost more than it will save. This is known as the **"sunk cost fallacy."**

- ➢ **Framing Effect**: How information is presented can have an impact on how judgment and decision-making are made.

- ➢ The **gambler's fallacy** is the idea that previous events have an impact on future probabilities in independent random events.

> The sensation of being a fake despite one's obvious accomplishments and success is known as **impostor syndrome**.

> **Recency Effect**: The propensity to recall information best when it has been presented recently.

> **Primacy Effect**: The propensity to recall information better when it is offered early on than when it is presented later.

> The propensity to regard something more highly just because one owns it is known as the **Endowment Effect**.

DID YOU KNOW???

> Glossophobia is the term for the dread of public speaking.

> Peer pressure is the psychological phenomena when individuals adhere to the conduct of their group.

> The term "serial position effect" refers to the propensity to recall the first and last items in a list.

> Affective reasoning is the process of making conclusions based more on feelings than on reason.

> Mirroring is the act of imitating the words or gestures of others.

> Affective forecasting error is the failure to foretell future emotional state.

> The bystander effect is the idea that individuals are more inclined to assist others in need if they are alone themselves.

> The false consensus effect is the propensity to overestimate the degree to which people share our

opinions and actions.

➢ The term "flashbulb memory effect" refers to the tendency for people to recall emotionally charged situations more vividly.

➢ Confirmation bias is the tendency to look for evidence that supports our preconceived notions.

➢ The self-serving bias is the propensity to blame outside forces for our shortcomings and internal variables for our accomplishments.

➢ Projecting our own negative characteristics onto other people is a psychological process.

➢ The sunk cost fallacy refers to the practice of pursuing a course of action or decision in the face of fresh information that suggests it may be incorrect.

➢ Loss aversion is the propensity to respond more strongly to the loss of something than to the acquisition of something as valuable.

➢ The illusion of control is the idea that we have greater influence over events than we actually do. Suppression is the act of not thinking about something that makes you uncomfortable.

> Social anxiety is the deliberate avoidance of social situations out of a fear of being judged.

> Obedience is the state in which individuals obey commands from superiors notwithstanding moral objections.

> Optimism bias is the propensity to overestimate the likelihood that good things will happen to us.

> The endowment effect is the psychological concept that states people appreciate things more highly just because they own them.

> Diffusion of responsibility is the propensity to be less willing to give assistance when others are around.

> The fundamental attribution fallacy is the tendency to attribute our own conduct to outside factors while attributing the actions of others to their character.

> The recency effect is the propensity to recall the final item in a series the best.

- Counterfactual thinking refers to the phenomena of feeling regret over past decisions.

- The mere exposure effect refers to the psychological propensity to choose familiar objects over unknown ones.

- Apophenia is the term used to describe people's propensity to see a link between seemingly unconnected occurrences.

- Reinforcement learning is the propensity to repeat actions that have produced favorable results in the past.

- Social support seeking is the inclination to look for social support when things are difficult.

- Egocentric bias refers to the tendency of evaluating people according to our personal experiences and prejudices.

- Biased interpretation refers to the psychological process of processing confusing information in a way that validates our preexisting ideas.

LESSER KNOWN FACTS ABOUT PART OF THE BODY HUMAN

Here are interesting and lesser-known facts about parts of the human body:

* The **liver** is the only internal organ that can regrow even after having up to 75% of its tissue removed.

* The **tonsils** serve as the immune system's first line of defense by capturing germs that enter through the mouth or nose.

* **Spleen:** Holds white blood cells and platelets, filters blood, and recycles old red blood cells.

* Even though it's frequently written off as vestigial, the **appendix** may be important for gut flora.

* **Vomeronasal Organ**, also known as **Jacob's Organ**: Although its use in humans is still up for question, this organ may be able to detect pheromones in certain individuals.

- ❖ **Melatonin**, a hormone that controls sleep-wake cycles, is produced by the pineal gland.

- ❖ The **inner ear's** spiral-shaped cochlea is the organ in charge of translating sound waves into nerve impulses.

- ❖ The **retina** is made up of rod and cone photoreceptor cells, which are used to perceive color and light.

- ❖ The bones of your fingers and toes are called **phalanges**.

- ❖ **Lacrimal glands**: secrete tears to maintain ocular moisture and aid in infection prevention.

- ❖ **Adipose tissue** insulates and cushions the body while storing energy as fat.

- ❖ **Thymus**: The immune system's key organ where T-cell maturation occurs.

- ❖ The colored portion of the eye called the **iris** regulates the pupil's diameter and, in turn, the quantity of light that reaches the retina.

- ❖ The **hypothalamus** is a little area of the brain that controls hormones and preserves homeostasis.

- ❖ **Uvula**: The little fleshy appendage at the rear of the throat used for swallowing and speaking.

- ❖ The tongue is supported by the **Hyoid Bone**, a U-shaped neck bone that is independent of all other bones.

- ❖ **Sternum**: Often referred to as the breastbone, it guards the lungs and heart.

- ❖ The **medulla oblongata** regulates blood pressure, heart rate, and respiration, among other autonomic processes.

- ❖ **Clavicle**: The bone that joins the arm to the body is also referred to as the collarbone.

- ❖ **Alveoli**: The lungs' tiny air sacs used for gas exchange.

- ❖ **Islets of Langerhans**: Groups of cells in the pancreas that are responsible for glucagon and insulin production.

❖ The **epiglottis** is a cartilaginous flap that covers the windpipe after swallowing, keeping food from going into the lungs.

❖ **Eustachian Tube**: Assists in balancing pressure by joining the middle ear and nasopharynx.

❖ The thick band of tissue that supports the arch at the bottom of the foot is called the **plantar fascia**.

❖ The **skin's Pacinian Corpuscles** are the nerve terminals that give rise to pressure and vibration sensation.

❖ The area of the brain that controls voluntary movement and balance is called the **cerebellum**.

❖ The **periosteum** is a thick covering of vascular connective tissue that surrounds the bones, with the exception of the joint surfaces.

❖ **Cerebrospinal fluid** is produced by a network of cells in the brain ventricles known as the choroid plexus.

DIDYOU KNOW????

- ❖ The stapes bone, which is found in the middle ear, is the smallest bone in the human body.

- ❖ The number of muscles in the human body is about 650.

- ❖ An adult human has between five and six liters of blood on average.

- ❖ The human body's largest organ is the skin.

- ❖ 75% of the human brain is made of water.

- ❖ The skeleton of an adult human has 206 bones.

- ❖ The only area of the human body devoid of blood flow is the cornea.

- ❖ Everybody has a distinct fingerprint set.

- ❖ There are approximately 37.2 trillion cells in the human body.

- ❖ There are roughly 8,000 taste buds on the tongue. Every day, your heart beats roughly 100,000 times.

- ❖ An adult typically has 2.5 million sweat glands.

- ❖ The average person can create between one and one and a half liters of saliva every day.

- ❖ The liver is the biggest organ in the human body.

- ❖ Your bones are continually being rebuilt and disassembled.

- ❖ There are roughly 10 million distinct colors that the human eye can discern between.

- ❖ Approximately 206 bones make up an adult's body, whereas newborns have about 270 bones.

- ❖ The masseter, or chewing muscle, is the strongest muscle in the human body in relation to its size.

- ❖ On average, a person's scalp contains 100,000 hair follicles.

* The frequency range in which the human body can detect sound is 20 Hz to 20,000 Hz.

* An estimated 1 trillion distinct smells can be detected by the human nose.

* The sartorius, which extends from the hip to the knee, is the longest muscle in the human body.

* A person's body is composed of 60% water.

* Every few days, the lining of your stomach is replaced to stop it from digesting itself.

* In adults, the small intestine measures around 22 feet in length.

* A person's taste buds, which range from 12,000 to 15,000, are replaced every one to two weeks.

* Hair is the tissue that grows fastest in the human body.

* Approximately two liters of mucus are produced daily by your body to coat and shield your respiratory system.

❖ Similar to fingerprints, the iris of each individual eye is unique.

❖ A person's blink rate is typically between 15 and 20 per minute.

LESSER KNOWN FACTS ABOUT SPORT

Here are interesting and lesser-known facts about sports:

➢ **Oldest Sport**: With roots in prehistoric Mesopotamia and Egypt, wrestling is regarded as one of the oldest sports.

➢ **Longest Tennis contest**: John Isner and Nicolas Mahut's three-day, 11-hour, 5-minute contest at

➢ **Wimbledon 2010** stands as the record for the longest tennis match.

➢ **Soccer's quickest Goal**: In a Saudi Arabian league game, Nawaf Al Abed scored the quickest goal in history 2.8 seconds after the game's opening kick.

➢ **Olympic Torch Relay**: For the 1936 Berlin Games, the Nazis instituted the Olympic torch relay for the first time.

➢ **First Female Olympic Champion**: Hélène de Pourtalès won the 1900 sailing competition, making history as the first female Olympian.

- ➢ **Longest Winning Streak**: Jahangir Khan, a squash player from Pakistan, has won 555 straight matches, the longest winning streak in professional sports.

- ➢ **NBA Game with the greatest Scoring Total**: The 1983 NBA game between the Detroit Pistons and the Denver Nuggets had the greatest scoring total, with 370 points.

- ➢ The youngest Olympic medallist was **Dimitrios Loundras**, who took home a bronze medal in gymnastics in 1896 at the age of ten.

- ➢ **First Super Bowl**: The Green Bay Packers defeated the Kansas City Chiefs in the inaugural Super Bowl, which took place in 1967.

- ➢ **Baseball's Perfect Game**: When a pitcher (or pitchers) retires all 27 batters without allowing any to reach base, it is called a perfect game.

- ➢ **Most World Cup Wins**: With five championships, Brazil now owns the record for the most FIFA World Cup wins.

- ➢ The **record-breaking** professional baseball game took eight hours and twenty-five minutes to finish, spanning thirty-three innings.

- ➢ The first marathon was run by the Greek soldier **Pheidippides**, who covered a distance of about 26 miles, running from Marathon to Athens.

- ➢ **Olympic Rings**: Africa, the Americas, Asia, Europe, and Oceania are the five inhabited continents that are represented by the five Olympic rings.

- ➢ **First Black NFL Coach**: In 1920, Fritz Pollard and Bobby Marshall were the league's first African American players.

- ➢ **First Modern Olympics**: In 1896, Athens hosted the first modern Olympic Games.

- ➢ **Fastest 100-Meter Sprint**: Set in 2009, Usain Bolt's time of 9.58 seconds is the record for the fastest 100-meter sprint.

- ➢ **Hockey Puck History**: Frozen cow dung was used to make the original hockey pucks.

- **Alan Shepard**, an astronaut, struck a golf ball on the moon in 1971 while on the Apollo 14 mission.

- **Oldest Major League Baseball ballpark:** Founded in 1912 and home to the Boston Red Sox, Fenway Park is the oldest ballpark in Major League Baseball.

- **Tour de France:** Founded in 1903, the Tour de France is the world's oldest and most esteemed cycling competition.

- The **record-breaking longest boxing** battle took place in 1893 and lasted 110 rounds, totaling 7 hours and 19 minutes.

- **First Woman to Run Boston Marathon**: In 1967, Kathrine Switzer became the first registered female entrant to run the Boston Marathon.

- **Heaviest Boxing Champion**: The heaviest boxing world champion in history is Nikolai Valuev, who weighs more than 320 pounds.

- **Olympic Gold Medals**: Only roughly 6 grams of gold make up the majority of Olympic gold medals, which are comprised of silver.

➢ The inaugural African **American Wimbledon champion** was none other than Althea Gibson, who claimed the championship in 1957.

➢ **Most Olympic Medals**: With a total of 28, Michael Phelps is the record holder for the most Olympic medals.

➢ **Fastest Land mammal**: The cheetah, which is comparable to sprinters like Usain Bolt, can attain brief bursts of speed of up to 75 mph, making it the fastest land mammal.

➢ **First Winter Olympics**: In 1924, Chamonix, France, hosted the first Winter Olympics.

➢ **Women's Professional Soccer League**: Established in 2001, the Women's United Soccer Association (WUSA) is the country's first professional women's soccer league.

DID YOU KNOW???

- The Summer and Winter Olympics alternate every two years, with the Olympic Games taking place every four years.

- There are 32 panels on the soccer ball used in professional games.

- For singles matches, a typical tennis court measures 78 feet long by 27 feet broad.

- A homerun in baseball is defined as hitting the ball out of the playing field into fair territory.

- 263.4 km/h (163.7 mph) is the world record for the fastest serve in tennis.

- A golf drive that is 510 yards (466 meters) long has ever been recorded.

- The Basketball Association of America (BAA) was the name under which the NBA was first established on June 6, 1946.

- ➢ In hockey, three goals in one game is referred to as a "hat-trick."

- ➢ Wilt Chamberlain holds the record for most points scored by a single player in an NBA game with 100.

- ➢ The breaststroke and dolphin kick were combined to create the butterfly stroke in swimming.

- ➢ A marathon is officially 26.2 miles (42.195 kilometers) long.

- ➢ First contested in 1967, the Super Bowl is the National Football League's (NFL) championship game.

- ➢ A "try" is worth five points in rugby, and a conversion kick that comes after a try is worth two points.

- ➢ Hakan Şükür scored the fastest goal in soccer 2.4 seconds into the game.

- ➢ In cricket, a batsman who is out without making any runs is referred to as a "duck."

➢ An annual men's multiple-stage bicycle race, mostly conducted in France, is called the Tour de France.

➢ Played over three days, the longest tennis match in history lasted 11 hours and five minutes.

➢ The end zone in American football is located ten yards deep.

➢ Just Fontaine held the record for the most goals scored by a single player in a World Cup competition in 1958 with eight.

➢ A "set" in volleyball refers to a tactic used to pass the ball to a teammate so they can attack.

➢ The Detroit Pistons and Denver Nuggets scored 186 points in a game that holds the record for the highest scoring NBA game ever played in 1983.

➢ A score of two strokes below par on a single hole is referred to as a "eagle" in golf.

➢ The decathlon in track and field consists of ten events, such as throwing, running, and jumping.

- Over 230 mph (370 km/h) is the fastest recorded speed in a Formula 1 vehicle worldwide.

- With 114,000 seats, the Rungrado 1st of May Stadium in North Korea is the biggest football stadium in the world.

- A "birdie" is the shuttlecock used in badminton games.

- In basketball, dribbling is the act of repeatedly bouncing the ball while in motion.

- In terms of games played, a 70-game match at Wimbledon in 2010 was the longest tennis match ever.

- A "penalty kick" is given in soccer when a foul is committed inside the penalty area.

- A perfect game of 300 is the best score ever attained in a professional bowling match.

LESSER KNOWN FACTS ABOUT LIFE

Here are interesting and lesser-known facts about life:

- **Abiogenesis** is the hypothesis that life evolved naturally from non-living substances, albeit the precise steps involved are yet unknown.

- The majority of life on Earth is derived from **photosynthesi**s, the process by which plants transform light energy into chemical energy.

- **Extremophiles** are organisms that live in harsh conditions, like acidic hot springs, deep-sea hydrothermal vents, and Antarctic ice.

- The ability of some organisms, such as fireflies and deep-sea life, to produce light through chemical processes is known as **bioluminescence**.

- The trillions of bacteria that reside in and on the human body and are essential to immunity, digestion, and general health are known as the **human microbiome.**

- The scientific hypothesis known as "cell theory" holds that cells, the fundamental building block of life, make up every living thing.

- **Endosymbiotic Theory**: The theory that larger cells ingested the free-living bacteria that gave rise to mitochondria and chloroplasts.

- **DNA** is a molecule that contains genetic information and was identified in 1953 by Francis Crick and James Watson.

- **CRISPR**: A novel gene-editing technique with potential uses in agriculture and medicine that enables precise DNA alterations.

- **Epigenetics**: The study of chemical changes that control gene expression without altering the DNA sequence.

- **Artificial intelligence** is the creation of computer programs that are capable of learning and making decisions—tasks that normally require human intelligence.

- The creation of materials, structures, and systems that are modeled by biological processes and organisms is known as **biomimicry.**

❖ The study of how evolutionary theories account for the composition and operation of the human mind is known as **evolutionary psychology**.

❖ **Mirror neurons**: These neurons, which may underlie empathy and learning, fire when a person performs an activity and when they witness someone else perform the same action.

❖ Named after its discovery on the Indonesian island of Flores, **Homo Floresiensis** is a species of diminutive, prehistoric humans sometimes known as **"hobbits."**

❖ **Panspermia** is the theory that life on Earth might have come from chemical precursors of life found in space or microbes.

❖ Significant in the development of bacteria, horizontal gene transfer is the transfer of genetic material between organisms other than by vertical transmission (parent to child).

❖ **Ecosystems** are groups of living things that interact with their surroundings to create intricate webs of dependency.

* ❖ The global ecological system that includes all life forms and its interactions with the atmosphere, hydrosphere, and lithosphere is known as the **biosphere.**

* ❖ The study of quantum phenomena in biological systems, including photosynthesis and enzyme activity, is known as **quantum biology**.

* ❖ **Antibiotic Resistance**: A major obstacle to modern medicine is the capacity of bacteria to generate defense mechanisms against the effects of medicines.

* ❖ **Synthetic biology**: the process of creating novel biological components, tools, and systems for practical applications; frequently, this involves genetic engineering.

* ❖ Cloning is the technique of creating artificially or naturally occurring individuals of an organism that are **genetically identical.**

* ❖ **Symbiosis**: The mutually beneficial interaction of two distinct species that live in close physical proximity.

- ❖ **Fracking**, also known as **hydraulic fracturing**, is a deep-sea resource extraction technique that has a major impact on the environment and ecology.

- ❖ **Biodiversity**: The variety and unpredictability of life on Earth, essential to human well-being and environmental resilience.

- ❖ The geological era known as the "**Anthropocene**" is said to have been defined by a major human influence on Earth's ecosystems and geology.

- ❖ Regardless of how useful they may be to humans, all living things and their natural environments have intrinsic value, according to the philosophy of biocentrism.

- ❖ James Lovelock postulated the "**Gaia Hypothesis**," which holds that the Earth and its biological processes function as a single, enormous organism.

DID YOU KNOW???

- A typical person will wait for red lights to turn green for around six months of their lives.

- Every year, humans lose over 1.5 pounds of skin, which adds to home dust.

- Only a small portion of the 70,000 ideas you have every day are actively retained.

- Only humans cry emotional tears. All other animals do not.

- Scents are known to bring back strong memories, and a person's sense of smell and memory are connected.

- A taste bud's lifespan is typically between 10 and 14 days.

- Around 300 bones make up an adult human, but by the time they reach adulthood, only 206 remain since some bones have fused together.

- Approximately 650 muscles in the human body are involved in posture maintenance and movement.

❖ The human body comprises approximately 37.2 trillion cells on average for an adult.

❖ With an annual growth rate of almost 6 inches, hair is the tissue in the human body that grows the fastest.

❖ The patterns on your tongue and your fingerprints are exclusive to you.

❖ There are roughly 10 million distinct colors that the human eye can discern between.

❖ Approximately 100,000 heartbeats every day, or 2,000 gallons of blood, are produced by an adult's heart.

❖ Your skeleton is continually reassembling; the complete structure needs to be replaced about every ten years.

❖ Over the course of a lifetime, the average person will walk 100,000 miles, or four times around the planet.

❖ The one to one and a half quarts of saliva that humans produce each day help with digestion and dental health.

- ❖ The stapes bone, located in the middle ear and roughly the size of a rice grain, is the smallest bone in the human body.

- ❖ Sleeping takes up around one-third of a human's life, or roughly 25 years if one lives to be 75 years old.

- ❖ Your skin makes up around 16% of your total weight and is your largest organ.

- ❖ Since water makes up around 60% of the human body, staying hydrated is essential for good health.

- ❖ The cornea is the only tissue in the human body that gets its oxygen straight from the atmosphere without the need for blood.

- ❖ A person's "biological clock" affects their hormone synthesis, sleep cycles, and other physiological functions.

- ❖ Though not all of the 5 million hair follicles on average create hair that is visible.

- ❖ About 80% of flavor originates in your nose, and your sense of taste and smell are tightly related.

* About two liters of mucus are produced daily by the human body to coat and protect the respiratory system.

* The typical person blinks between 15 and 20 times each minute, which keeps their eyes moist and clear of particles.

* The vestibular system in the inner ear, which aids in staying upright and coordinating movement, maintains a person's feeling of balance.

* The skin, the largest organ in your body, is home to a sophisticated nerve network that gives you sensations of pain, pressure, and temperature.

* The majority of the sound frequencies used in human speech fall within the range that the human body can detect, which extends from as low as 20 Hz to as high as 20,000 Hz.

LESSER KNOWN FACTS ABOUT NEW BORN BABBIES

Here are interesting and lesser-known facts about newborn babies:

➢ **More Bones**: A newborn's about 300 bones will fuse together to form 206 by the time they reach maturity.

➢ The soft areas on a baby's head called **fontanelles** allow the skull to bend during birth and brain development.

➢ **Vision**: Newborns like patterns with strong contrast and can only see objects that are 8 to 12 inches distant.

➢ **Taste and Smell**: Newborns have highly developed senses of taste and smell, and they can identify their mother's aroma in a few of days.

➢ **Hearing**: Unborn children are able to distinguish their mother's voice and hear in the womb.

- ➢ **Reflexes**: Newborns are born with a variety of reflexes, such as the grip, rooting, and Moro (startle) reflexes.

- ➢ **Heart Rate**: A newborn's heart beats between 120 and 160 beats per minute, which is significantly quicker than an adult's.

- ➢ **Lanugo**: A newborn's fine hair covering its body, which typically goes away in the first few weeks of life.

- ➢ **Meconium**: A newborn's first feces, made up of substances consumed in the womb, is thick, viscous, and dark green.

- ➢ **Sleep Patterns**: Newborns sleep for as long as 16–17 hours every day, but only in little 2-4 hour stretches.

- ➢ **Weight Loss**: In the first few days after birth, it's common for babies to lose up to 10% of their birth weight, which they typically restore by the second week.

- ➢ **No Tears**: Although newborns scream, their tear ducts are still developing, therefore they don't cry very much.

- ➢ **Skin**: Newborn skin may have little white pimples known as milia or seem red and blotchy.

- ➢ **Breastfeeding:** The content of breast milk varies over time to suit the baby's nutritional demands.

- ➢ **Umbilical Cord Stump**: The stump of the umbilical cord falls off within the first one to three weeks.

- ➢ **Jaundice**: Jaundice, or yellowing of the skin and eyes, is a common condition in neonates that typically goes away on its own.

- ➢ **Immune System**: Breast milk and the placenta allow babies to acquire antibodies from their mother, which gives them first immunity.

- ➢ **Weight Gain**: During the first six months of life, after the initial weight loss, babies usually gain one to two pounds per month.

- ➢ **Head Circumference**: At birth, a baby's head makes up roughly 25% of their body length, whereas an adult's head makes up roughly 12%.

- ➢ **Growth Spurts**: Between two to three weeks, six weeks, and three months, newborns typically go through fast growth spurts.

- ➢ **Grasp Reflex**: Infants can grasp a finger firmly and have a strong grip.

- ➢ **Temperature Regulation**: Newborns require assistance to stay warm or cool because they have trouble controlling their body temperature.

- ➢ The sucking reflex is a vital feeding response that aids in sucking and swallowing for infants.

- ➢ **Breathing Patterns**: It is typical for newborns to have irregular breathing patterns, with pauses of up to 10 seconds.

- ➢ Babies breathe mainly via their noses, which helps them to feed.

- ➢ **Taste Preferences**: Breast milk is naturally sweet since newborns have a predilection for sweet flavors.

- ➢ **Sleep Cycles**: A newborn's sleep cycle is 50–60 minutes shorter than an adult's, which causes them to wake up more frequently.

➢ **Diaper Changes**: Because they urinate and stool frequently, newborns can go through eight to twelve diaper changes in a day.

➢ **Fast Development**: During the first year of life, the size of the brain approximately doubles.

➢ **Social Smiling**: Around 6 to 8 weeks of age, babies usually begin smiling in reaction to stimuli such as their parent's face or voice.

DID YOU KNOW???

➢ Soon after birth, newborns can identify their mother's voice.

➢ Approximately 70 reflexes, including the grip and rooting reflexes, are present in newborns.

➢ Infants are able to discriminate between flavors and have a preference for sweet ones.

➢ The many plates that make up a baby's skull allow for growth and flexibility right after birth.

➢ Compared to adults, babies are born with about 100 billion extra neurons, which are later pruned as they grow.

➢ Due to their innate predilection for faces, newborns frequently focus on human faces first.

➢ A newborn typically sleeps for 16–17 hours per day, often for shorter bursts of 2-4 hours.

➢ The first smile a newborn makes, which can happen as early as six weeks, is usually a reflex rather than a social gesture.

- ➤ Because they can only see objects 8 to 12 inches in front of them, newborns are best able to focus on the face of a caregiver.

- ➤ A newborn's white, waxy skin coating, known as the vernix caseosa, aids in shielding the child from germs and after delivery.

- ➤ During the first few days of life, newborns usually lose around 10% of their birth weight; but, within two weeks, they restore it.

- ➤ Newborns possess a complete palette of taste buds, enabling them to discriminate between sweet, sour, bitter, and salty tastes.

- ➤ Because many of their bones fuse together as they grow, newborns have more bones than adults.

- ➤ At birth, the average baby's head circumference measures about 35 centimeters, or roughly 25% of their whole length.

- ➢ From the womb, babies can begin to identify and react to familiar voices and noises.

- ➢ A baby's fontanelles, or soft areas on its skull, provide flexible movement and brain development during birth.

- ➢ Due to their inability to regulate their body temperature, newborns rely on their caregivers to keep them warm.

- ➢ Because of their highly developed sense of smell, newborns can identify their mother's aroma very soon after birth.

- ➢ Babies require a lot of sleep from birth in order to maintain their rapid brain growth.

- ➢ A newborn often goes through 8 to 12 diapers in a day because of their frequent eating schedule and small stomach.

- ➢ Newborns can grab onto items with surprising strength for their size and have a strong grasp reflex.

➢ After birth, the umbilical cord stump often falls off in one to three weeks, exposing the belly button.

➢ Startle reflexes, which are erratic jerking movements in newborns, are common and eventually go away.

➢ During the first few months of life, the baby's vision steadily gets better, and it begins to recognize colors and dimension.

➢ Since a newborn's immune system is still growing, antibodies from the mother are mostly obtained through the placenta and breast milk.

➢ Over time, the composition of breast milk varies to suit the changing nutritional needs of the developing infant.

➢ Because they can only breathe through their noses, newborns frequently "breathe through their noses" to make feeding easier.

➢ A baby's fontanelles, or soft areas on their skull, gradually shut as they get older. By the time the baby is 18 to 24 months old, the anterior fontanelle has closed.

➢ As they begin to learn how to communicate, newborns frequently make a range of noises, such as coos, gurgles, and cries.

➢ The rooting reaction is essential for nursing because it enables babies to tilt their heads toward the source of stimulation, such as a nipple.

LESSER KNOWN FACTS ABOUT CLOTHING AND SHOES

Here are interesting and lesser-known facts about clothes and shoes:

- ❖ **Oldest Shoes**: Sandals discovered in Fort Rock Cave, Oregon, which date back more than 10,000 years are the oldest shoes ever discovered.

- ❖ **Origin of Hills**: Men first wore high heels in the tenth century to help keep their stirrups in place while they rode horses.

- ❖ **The invention of jeans**: In 1873, Levi Strauss and Jacob Davis created denim pants as a sturdy workwear option for miners.

- ❖ **Little Black Dress**: The "little black dress," made famous by Coco Chanel in 1926, revolutionized women's fashion with its understated elegance and simplicity.

- ❖ A community of fans known as **"sneakerheads"** collects, trades, and venerates sneakers as status and cultural symbols.

- **T-shirts**: Originally worn as undergarments by American sailors in World War I, T-shirts have since become a mainstay of casual attire.

- A method of creating, sourcing, and manufacturing apparel that optimizes positive effects on individuals and communities while reducing negative effects on the environment is known as **ethical fashion**.

- **Bespoke tailoring** is the term used to describe clothes that are manufactured specifically to match the measurements and preferences of a person.

- **Fast fashion** is a business model that produces trendy clothing in large quantities quickly at a low cost; it is frequently condemned for its negative effects on the environment and on ethics.

- **Secondhand Clothes**: As a more environmentally friendly and socially conscious option to fast fashion, buying and selling old clothing has become more and more popular. It also encourages recycling.

- **Athleisure**: A fashion movement that allows sportswear to be worn on a daily basis and blends leisure and athletic styles.

- ❖ **Production of Silk:** To extract silk, one must unwind the cocoon in order to acquire a continuous thread. Silkworms generate silk.

- ❖ **Sustainable Fabrics:** Because they have less of an influence on the environment, materials including recycled polyester, hemp, bamboo, and organic cotton are gaining popularity.

- ❖ **Sneaker Technology**: For improved comfort and performance, contemporary sneakers frequently use cutting-edge materials and technologies like memory foam, air cushioning, and breathable textiles.

- ❖ **Uniforms:** Worn in businesses, schools, and military institutions, uniforms foster a sense of cohesion and belonging.

- ❖ **Dress codes** are socially constructed guidelines that specify what is suitable to wear in certain settings, such as formal occasions, the workplace, and places of worship.

- ❖ **Vintage Clothes:** Fashion aficionados and collectors favor clothing from earlier decades, which is frequently prized for its distinctive style and craftsmanship.

- ❖ **Fashion Weeks**: Important fashion shows where designers present their newest collections are held in major cities such as New York, Paris, Milan, and London.

- ❖ **Corsets:** Originally used primarily to shape the waist and body, corsets have become more fashionable than functional.

- ❖ Whitcomb Judson invented the zipper in 1893, and since then, it has revolutionized clothing fastening and become an essential component of fashion.

- ❖ **Footbinding**: A traditional Chinese custom in which young girls' feet were firmly bound to change their shape and become a status and beauty symbol.

- ❖ **Kilts:** Traditionally worn by Scottish women, kilts are knee-length skirts with rear pleats made of woolen fabric patterned in tartan.

- ❖ **Denim** is a durable cotton twill material that is most frequently connected to jeans and has evolved into a classic piece of clothing.

* **Hand-me-downs**: Clothing that is passed down from one person to another, frequently within families, encouraging sustainability and reuse.

* **Designer labels** are high-end clothing companies like Gucci, Chanel, and Louis Vuitton that are renowned for their exclusivity, elegance, and distinctive designs.

* **The history of buttons**: Though they have been used for thousands of years, the first buttons that are known to exist date to the Indus Valley Civilization, which flourished around 2000 BCE.

* **Wool:** Wool is a natural fiber made from sheep that is prized for its warmth, toughness, and moisture-absorbing capacity.

* A **capsule wardrobe** is a minimalist approach to clothing that consists of a small number of classic, adaptable pieces that can be worn in different ways to create several looks.

* **Innovations in Footwear**: Shoes have developed over time to incorporate a variety of specific designs for a range of sports, including dancing, hiking, and

jogging.

- ❖ **Cultural attire** is traditional apparel that reflects a culture's heritage and identity. It is frequently worn during festivals, ceremonies, and other important events.

LESSER KNOWN FACTS ABOUT FOOD AND DRINKS

The following lists are of fascinating and little-known facts about food, beverages, and their packaging:

❖ Tine is the term for a fork's prongs.

❖ Citric acid is the chemical component that gives lemons their acidic flavor.

❖ A wine specialist with a focus on wine and food pairings is known as a sommelier.

❖ Glass bottles are frequently formed by melting limestone, soda ash, and sand at a high temperature.

❖ Meat was the first food item to be cannily packaged in the early 1800s.

❖ The fifth basic taste, characterized as savory or meaty, is called umami.

❖ Canning was first popularized in the early 1800s by Nicolas Appert.

❖ At more than 2,600 pounds, the biggest pumpkin ever measured was found.

❖ Cork may be recycled and used again; it is extracted from the bark of cork oak trees.

❖ Liquids are heated to destroy bacteria during the pasteurization process, which bears Louis Pasteur's name.

❖ In the 1800s, Perrier became the first water to be sold in bottles for commercial use.

❖ Si Racha is the name of the Thai city where Sriracha sauce first appeared.

❖ Cheese's rind, or outside layer, enhances flavor and is frequently edible.

❖ The only food that never goes bad is honey, which has been shown to be edible in ancient Egyptian tombs.

- ❖ The pressure in carbonated drinks releases when a bottle opens, making the distinctive "pop" sound.

- ❖ After water, tea is the beverage that is drank worldwide the second most.

- ❖ In the past, the French word "gourmet" denoted a wine trader or taster.

- ❖ About 100 AD is when paper packaging was first used in ancient China.

- ❖ The word "cheddar" describes a particular kind of cheese as well as the English village where it first appeared.

- ❖ In 1990, the FDA started requiring food packaging to include a "nutrition facts" label.

- ❖ 1903 saw the patenting of peanut butter by Dr. John Harvey Kellogg.

- ❖ Coffee's bitter flavor is caused by substances known as chlorogenic acids and phenols.

- ❖ Using a hammer and chisel, the metal can was first opened in order to preserve food.

- ❖ Fermentation is the process used to make items like wine, beer, and sourdough bread.

- ❖ Food packaging's "best before" date denotes peak quality rather than safety.

- ❖ Tetra Paks were created in the 1950s to increase the liquid food's shelf life.

- ❖ To preserve color and texture, blanching is the practice of quickly boiling vegetables before freezing or canning.

- ❖ An "artisan" is a person who is proficient in creating food items by hand using age-old techniques.

- ❖ In2012, an Italian pizza weighing more than 51,000 pounds was created to become the largest in history.

- ❖ The word "smoothie" first used in reference to a creamy fruit drink in the 1960s.

LESSER KNOWN FACTS ABOUT MEDICAL

Here are interesting facts about medicine and medical science:

➢ An average person's heart beats 100,000 times every day.

➢ The femur is the longest bone in the human body.

➢ A typical human body has five to six liters of blood.

➢ The only tissue in the human body devoid of blood flow is the cornea.

➢ The human body's largest organ is the skin.

➢ The largest internal organ in the human body is the liver.

➢ There are approximately 86 billion neurons in the human brain.

- Every day, the kidneys filter about fifty gallons of blood.

- There are roughly 37.2 trillion cells in the human body.

- About 60% of an adult human's body is made up of water.

- In adults, the small intestine measures around 22 feet in length.

- There are roughly 2.5 million sweat glands on an average individual.

- An estimated 1 trillion distinct smells can be detected by the human nose.

- There are roughly 10 million distinct colors that the human eye can discern between.

- Every day, the heart pumps over 2,000 liters of blood. An estimated 1 to 1.5 liters of saliva are produced everyday by the human body.

- A taste bud's lifespan is typically between 10 and 14 days.

- Approximately 20% of the body's total oxygen and energy are used by the brain.

- When the human body is exposed to sunshine, vitamin D is produced.

- The spleen aids in blood filtration and red blood cell iron recycling.

- An adult typically possesses 32 teeth, divided into four categories: canines, molars, incisors, and premolars.

- The appendix is a tiny, tube-shaped structure that may be involved in immunological response but has no recognized vital function.

- There are 206 bones in the human body, starting at roughly 270 at birth.

- The thyroid gland is a gland in the neck that controls metabolism.

- The windpipe, or trachea, joins the throat and lungs and is approximately 4 inches long.

- The gluteus maximus is the largest muscle in the human body.

- On their scalp, adults typically contain 100,000 hair follicles.

- Often referred to as the "master gland," the pituitary controls the activity of other endocrine glands.

- The human body has the ability to produce endorphins, which are natural painkillers.

LESSER KNOWN FACTS ABOUT MUSIC

Here are interesting facts about music:

* There are 88 keys on the piano: 52 white and 36 black.

* A typical string quartet in an orchestra consists of one cello, one viola, and two violins.

* The phrase "a cappella" describes vocals that are performed without an instrument.

* The staff, which comprises of five lines and four spaces, is the most often used system of musical notation.

* The cello is played between the knees and is renowned for its rich, deep sound.

* An octave is defined as the interval of eight diatonic notes in music theory.

- A metronome is a tool used to time music at a predetermined speed.

- In music notation, "forte" refers to playing loudly.

- The Neanderthal flute, which was fashioned from a bird bone and is thought to be about 40,000 years old, is the oldest musical instrument ever discovered.

- The octave in Western music is divided into twelve equal sections by the twelve-tone scale.

- "Legato" refers to playing with a fluid, linked style that doesn't have any discernible note breaks.

- With thousands of pipes, the pipe organ is the biggest musical instrument in the world.

- Although the standard guitar has six strings, there are variants with seven, eight, nine, or more.

- "Staccato" describes a disengaged or isolated style of performing or singing.

- A piece of music that gradually increases in volume is called a "crescendo."

❖ A quick and energetic pace is indicated by the "Allegro" tempo marking.

❖ The viola has a richer, deeper sound than the violin and is slightly bigger.

❖ A moderate strolling pace is indicated by the "Andante" tempo marking.

❖ A "trill" is a fast alternation of two adjacent notes used as a musical embellishment.

❖ The notation "sforzando" (sfz) denotes a quick, intense stress on a note or chord.

❖ A brief musical motif or idea that appears repeatedly in a composition is called a "motif."

❖ A note that is performed or sung in jazz at a slightly lower pitch for expressive reasons is referred to as a "blue note."

❖ The mouth organ, sometimes referred to as the "harmonica," is operated by forcing air through
❖ perforations in a chamber made of reeds.

❖ "Ritardando" refers to progressively reducing a piece's tempo.

❖ "Dynamics" in music refers to changes in volume and intensity.

❖ A method known as "counterpoint" involves the harmonious combination of two or more melodic lines.

❖ A theme is introduced and subsequently developed through interlaced lines in a musical form called a "fugue."

❖ Kettle drums, sometimes referred to as "timpani," are percussion instruments with adjustable pitches.

❖ The set of frequencies at which a system vibrates inherently is referred to as the "harmonic series."

❖ In keyboard and string instruments, the "glissando" is a sliding motion that changes pitch.

LESSER KNOWN FACTS ABOUT HUMAN BRAINS

Here are intriguing facts about the brain and illusions:

➢ It weights roughly three pounds (1.4 kg) to be a human brain.

➢ There are roughly 86 billion neurons in the brain.

➢ Higher order brain processes like thought and action are controlled by the cerebral cortex, which is located on the outside of the brain.

➢ Approximately 20% of the body's total oxygen and energy are used by the brain.

➢ The left hemisphere of the brain is usually responsible for analytical and linguistic functions.

➢ Creativity and spatial intelligence are commonly linked to the right hemisphere of the brain.

➢ The hippocampus in the brain is essential for creating new memories.

75% of the brain is made of water.

- ➢ One area of the brain that is important in processing emotions like pleasure and fear is the amygdala.

- ➢ Image processing in the brain can happen in as little as 13 milliseconds.

- ➢ There are roughly 100 trillion synapses in the average brain.

- ➢ The number of connections in the brain exceeds the number of stars in the Milky Way galaxy.

- ➢ "Perceptual completion" refers to the process through which the brain completes the gaps in visual information.

- ➢ The "mirror neuron system" enables us to comprehend and imitate other people's behavior.

- ➢ Amputees who experience feelings in a missing limb are said to be experiencing the "phantom limb" phenomena.

- ➢ The brain's ability to alternate between perceiving two faces and a vase is illustrated by the "Rubin's Vase" illusion.

- ➢ Due to the direction of the arrows at the ends, two lines of similar length appear to differ in the "Müller-Lyer" illusion.

- ➢ One example of an impossibility that the brain perceives as a three-dimensional shape is the "Penrose Triangle."

- ➢ When you focus on a focal point, objects on the periphery of your vision disappear due to the "Troxler Effect."

- ➢ In the "Ebbinghaus Illusion," circles of varying diameters cause one to appear larger or smaller in relation to the circles around it.

- ➢ The "Kanizsa Triangle" illusion gives the impression that there is a white triangle when there isn't one.

- ➢ According to the "Gestalt Principles," the brain integrates or unifies visual parts into cohesive wholes.

- ➢ When a person is at rest and not paying attention to the outside world, the "default mode network" in the brain is activated.

- ➤ Because of its "plasticity," the brain can change and rearrange itself as we age.

- ➤ The "McGurk Effect" shows how opposing aural and visual signals can blend together when we are exposed to visual information.

- ➤ The "Ames Room" illusion distorts the perception of size by using a distorted room shape.

- ➤ The "Zöllner Illusion" is the phenomenon where lines with intersecting lines appear distorted.

- ➤ Due to their shadow environment, two squares of the same color appear different in the "Checker Shadow Illusion."

- ➤ Dreams are produced by the brain and are frequently a combination of recollections and imagined events.

- ➤ The brain's function in deciphering ambiguous visuals is demonstrated by the "Rubin's Vase" illusion, which can also be interpreted as a single vase or as two faces in profile.

LESSER KNOWN FACTS ABOU
HUMAN REACTION

The following fascinating facts about human emotions:

❖ The body gets ready to either face or escape a threat through the **"fight or flight"** reaction.

❖ A conditioned reflex known as the **"Pavlovian response"** occurs when a neutral stimulus starts to elicit a particular reaction in the body.

❖ Babies react with an infantile reflex known as the **"Moro reflex"** when they hear a loud noise or abrupt loss of support.

❖ A limb will tend to pull away from a painful stimulation due to the **"withdrawal reflex."**

❖ The **"orienting response"** draws attention to a new or noteworthy environmental stimulation.

❖ The **"gag reflex"** causes a coughing or choking reaction, which helps shield the airway from foreign things.

* ❖ The **"blush response"** is the dilatation of facial blood vessels brought on by emotional tension or humiliation.

* ❖ The **"tend and befriend"** response refers to a behavioral pattern in which people look for help from others while they are under stress.

* ❖ In the face of danger, the **"freezing response"** entails staying motionless and silent, frequently in order to avoid being discovered.

* ❖ The **"tickling response"** is a reaction to light touches on sensitive body parts that makes people chuckle and wriggle.

* ❖ A rapid reflexive movement in reply to an unexpected stimuli is known as a **"startle reaction."**

* ❖ The **"flight response"** refers to getting away from or away from a perceived threat or danger.

* ❖ The **"blush reflex"** is the reaction of embarrassed or aroused emotions to redden the cheeks.

- ❖ The **"orienting reflex"** draws attention to unfamiliar or significant environmental stimuli.

- ❖ A rapid reflexive movement is known as the **"startle reaction"** and it occurs in response to an unexpected input.

- ❖ In the face of danger, the **"freeze response"** entails staying motionless and silent, frequently in order to avoid being discovered.

- ❖ The **"tend-and-befriend"** response refers to a behavioral pattern in which people turn to others for help while they're under stress.

- ❖ The **"tickling reflex"** is a reaction to light touches on sensitive body parts that makes people chuckle and wriggle.

- ❖ A defense mechanism known as the **"withdrawal response"** pushes people away from potentially dangerous stimuli.

- ❖ The body gets ready for a perceived threat by triggering the **"fight-or-flight"** reaction.

❖ Babies have a reflex known as the "**Moro reflex**," which makes them startle when they suddenly lose assistance or hear loud noises.

❖ The "**orienting response**" draws attention to interesting or noteworthy environmental stimuli.

❖ The "**gag reflex**" causes a coughing or choking reaction, which helps shield the airway from foreign things.

❖ The "**blush response**" is the dilatation of facial blood vessels brought on by emotional tension or humiliation.

❖ A rapid contraction of the muscles occurs during the "**startle response**" in reaction to an abrupt sound or motion.

CONCLUSION

We are grateful that you have chosen to read **The Ultimate Book of Unusual Insights: Fascinating Lesser-Known Facts Across Nature, Science, and Human Experience**. I hope this book has filled you with amazement, happiness, and enlightenment.

I hope these facts spark your curiosity and help you gain a greater understanding of the hidden gems that make our planet so intriguing as you continue to explore the world around you. Never forget that there is always more to learn; thus, never stop researching, asking questions, and imparting your fresh perspectives to others.

Cheers to your exploration!

Sincerely,

SCOTT KELLER

GLOSSARY

- **Adaptation**: The process by which living things modify their existing environments or adapt to new ones.
- **Amygdala**: a part of the brain that deals with processing feelings like pleasure and fear.
- **Silly Reaction**: a reaction that causes redness in the face by dilation of the blood vessels, usually brought on by emotional stress or shame.
- The network of brain areas known as the **Default Mode Network** is active while the brain is at rest and not focusing on the outside world.
- **Ebbinghaus Illusion**: A optical illusion in which surrounding circles distort one's perception of a circle's size.
- **Fight or Flight Response**: An internal body reaction brought on by a perceived threat to life, an attack, or a damaging situation.
- **Gestalt Principles**: Visual perception theories that explain how individuals often combine visual components into cohesive wholes.
- A region of the brain called the hippocampus is involved in the creation of new memories
- **Interrobang**: a combination of an exclamation point and a question mark (?!).

- ❖ **Kanizsa Triangle**:An optical trick in which, even in the absence of an explicit drawing, a triangle is perceived.
- ❖ **The McGurk Effect**: a situation where competing auditory and visual impulses combine because of visual information influencing what we hear.
- ❖ **Mirror Neuron System**:A collection of specialized neurons that provide humans the ability to comprehend and imitate other people's movements.
- ❖ **Extra Reflex**: a primitive reaction that makes infants flinch at loud noises or abrupt losses of support.
- ❖ **Neurons**: The fundamental brain cells are specialized cells that use chemical and electrical impulses to communicate information.
- ❖ **Orienting Response**: An involuntary response that draws attention to a fresh or noteworthy stimuli.
- ❖ **Penrose Triangle**: A nonexistent item giving the appearance of being three-dimensional.
- ❖ **Perceptual Completion**: The process by which the mind completes some visual information that is absent.
- ❖ A phenomenon known as **"Phantom Limb"** occurs when amputees experience feelings in a missing limb.
- ❖ **Plasticity**: The brain's capacity for self-organization and adaptation.
- ❖ **Rubin's Vase**: An optical trick that seems to be two faces in profile or a vase.

APPENDIX

A. Further Reading

1. **Curious Nature:** Books that explore the natural world's marvels in greater detail.
2. **Brain Teasers**: Books delving into the secrets of psychology and the human brain.
3. **Human Behavior**: Comprehensive resources on the subtleties of human behavior.

B. Suggested Online Resources

1. Scientific American: www.scientificamerican.com;
2. National Geographic: www.nationalgeographic.com
3. Psychological Today:http://www.psychologicaltoday.com

C. Thought-provoking Documentaries

1. **Planet Earth**: A thorough examination of the environment.
2. **Brain Gamesp**; An animated series delving into the workings of the human brain.
3. An in-depth examination of neonatal behavior and development is provided in The Secret Life of Babies.

D. Practical Online Education

1. **Coursera**: Natural science, psychology, and nature courses.
2. **edX**:Behavior and brain science courses.
3. **Udemy**: Educational materials on a variety of fascinating subjects.

E. Recognitions

I would especially like to thank all the scientists, researchers, and educators whose findings and contributions have influenced the information in this book. We are really grateful for your commitment to revealing the world's hidden treasures.

F. Index